Filipina Girls

Hot Sexy Filipina Lingerie Girls Models Pictures

By **PHOTO ART LOVER**

Copyright © Filipina Girls

All rights reserved. No part of this document may be
Reproduced or transmitted in any form or by any means, electronic, mechanical, photocopying,
Recording, or otherwise, without prior written permission of photo art lover.

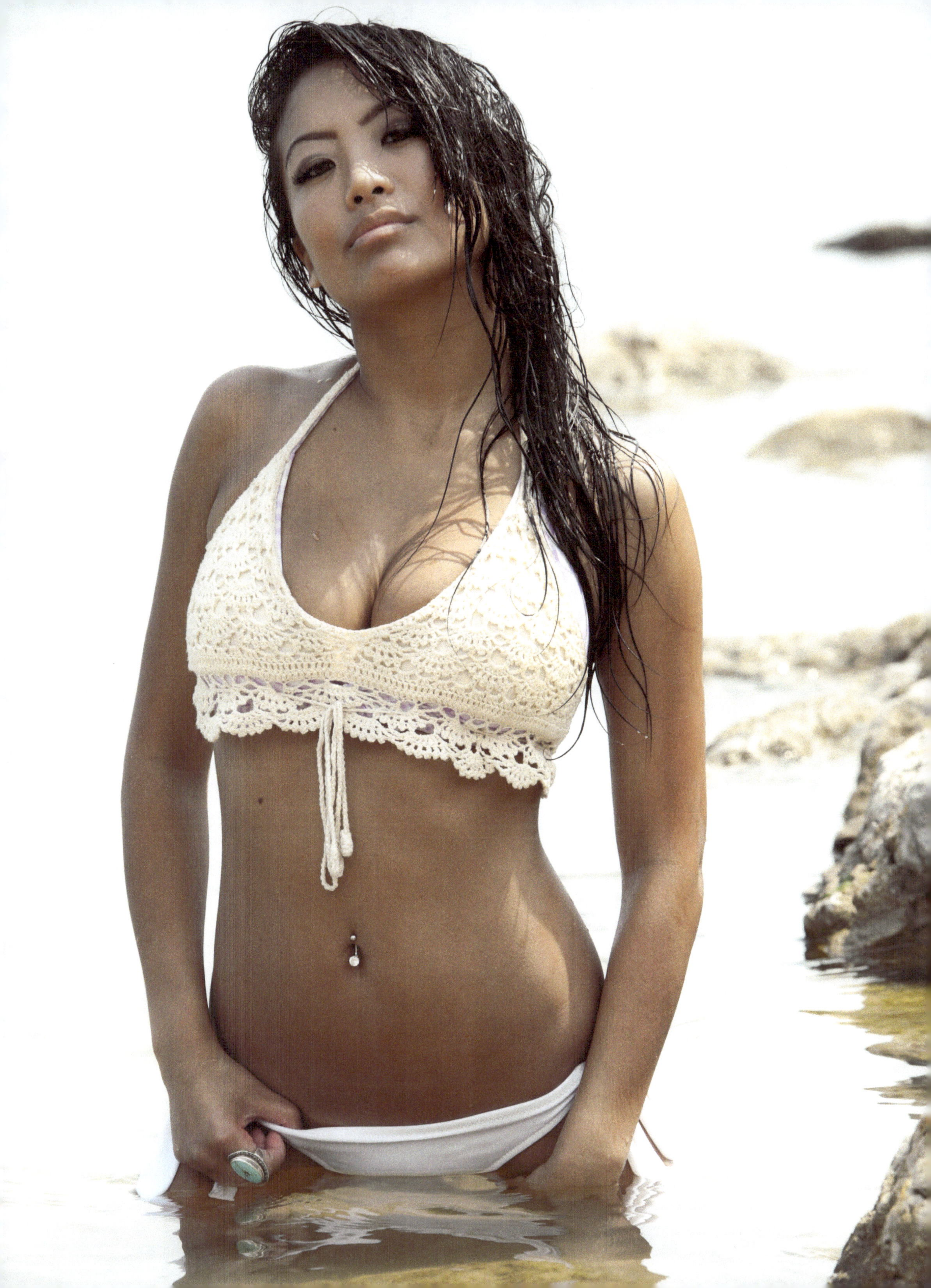

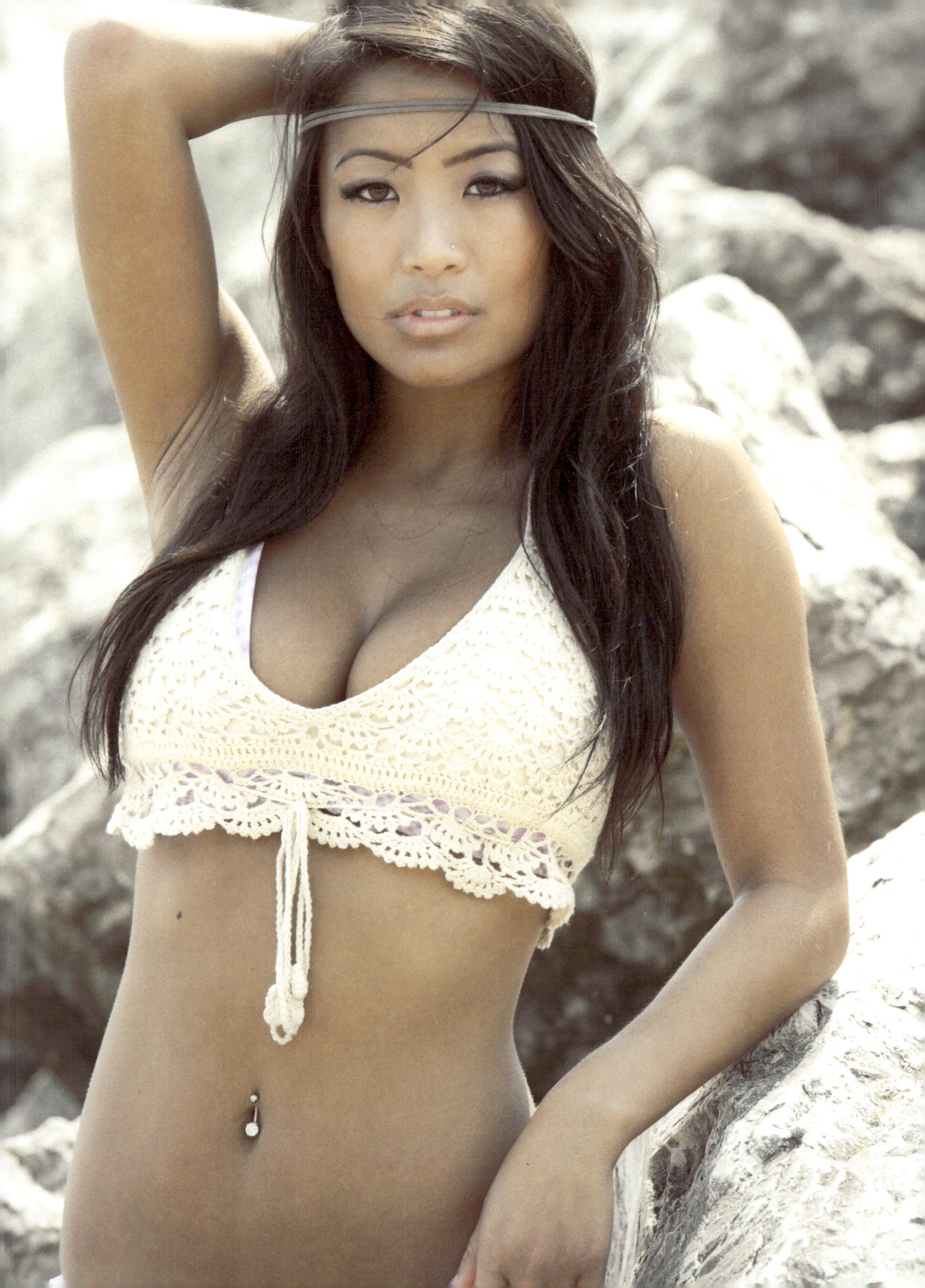

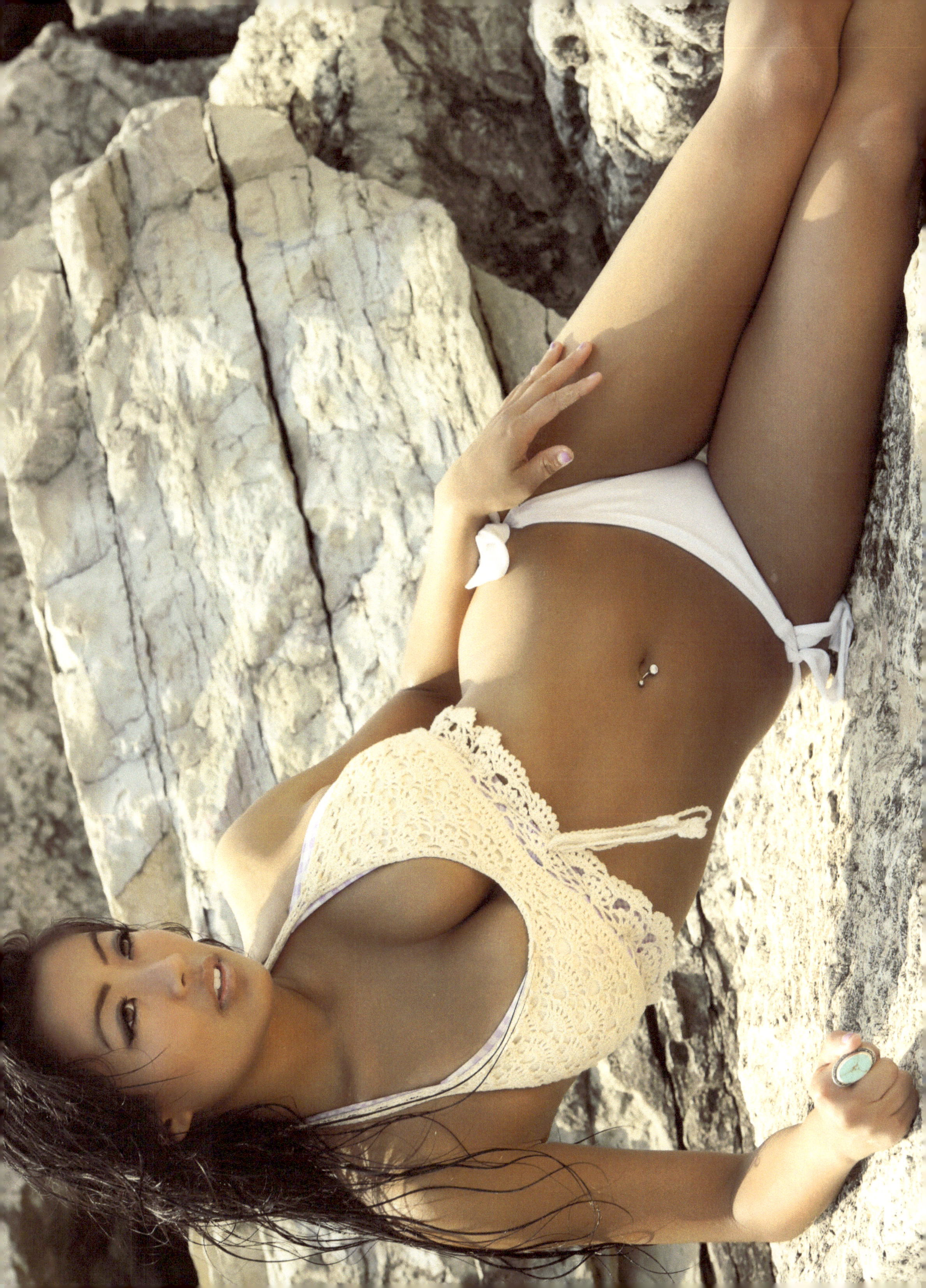

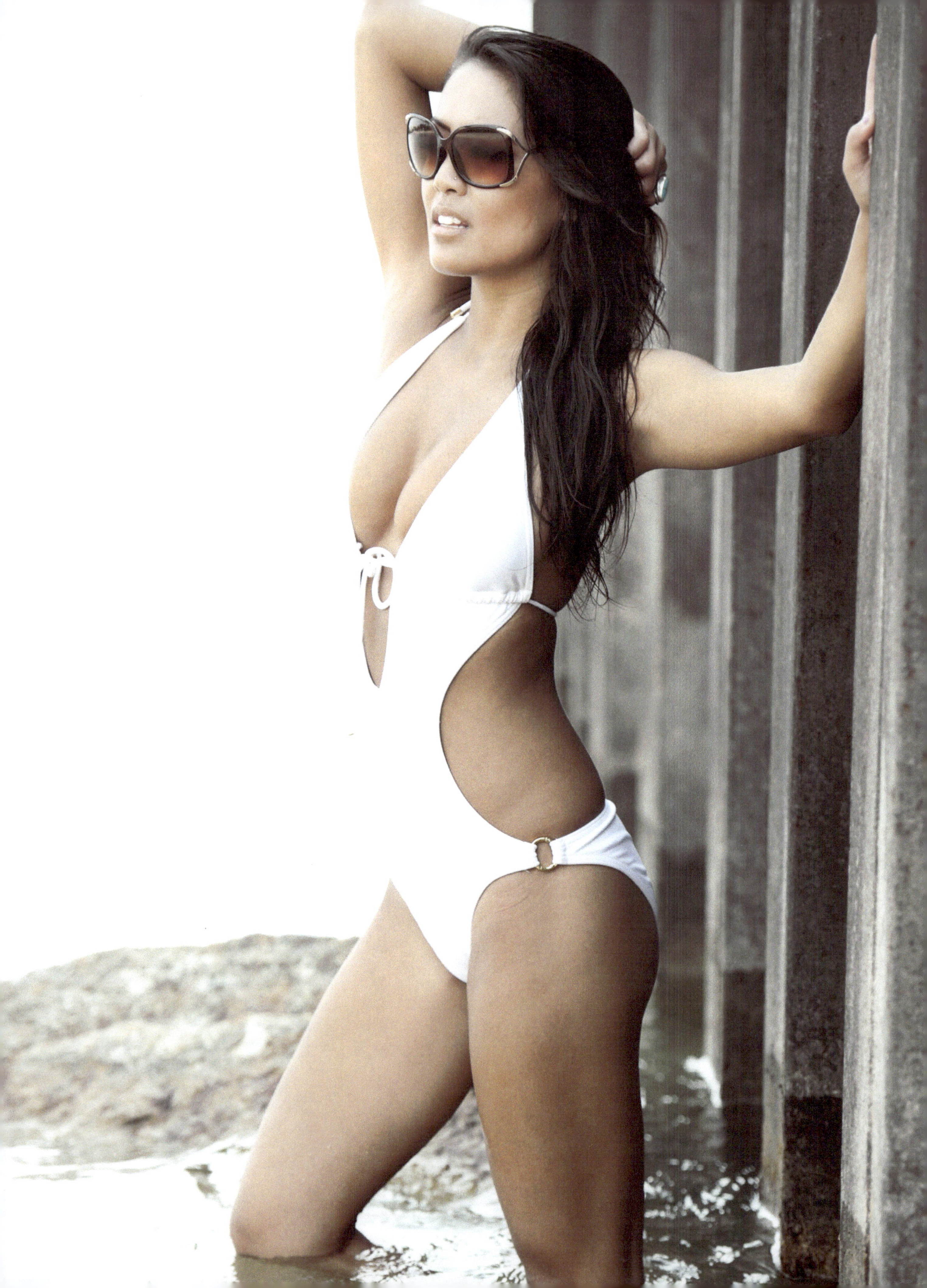

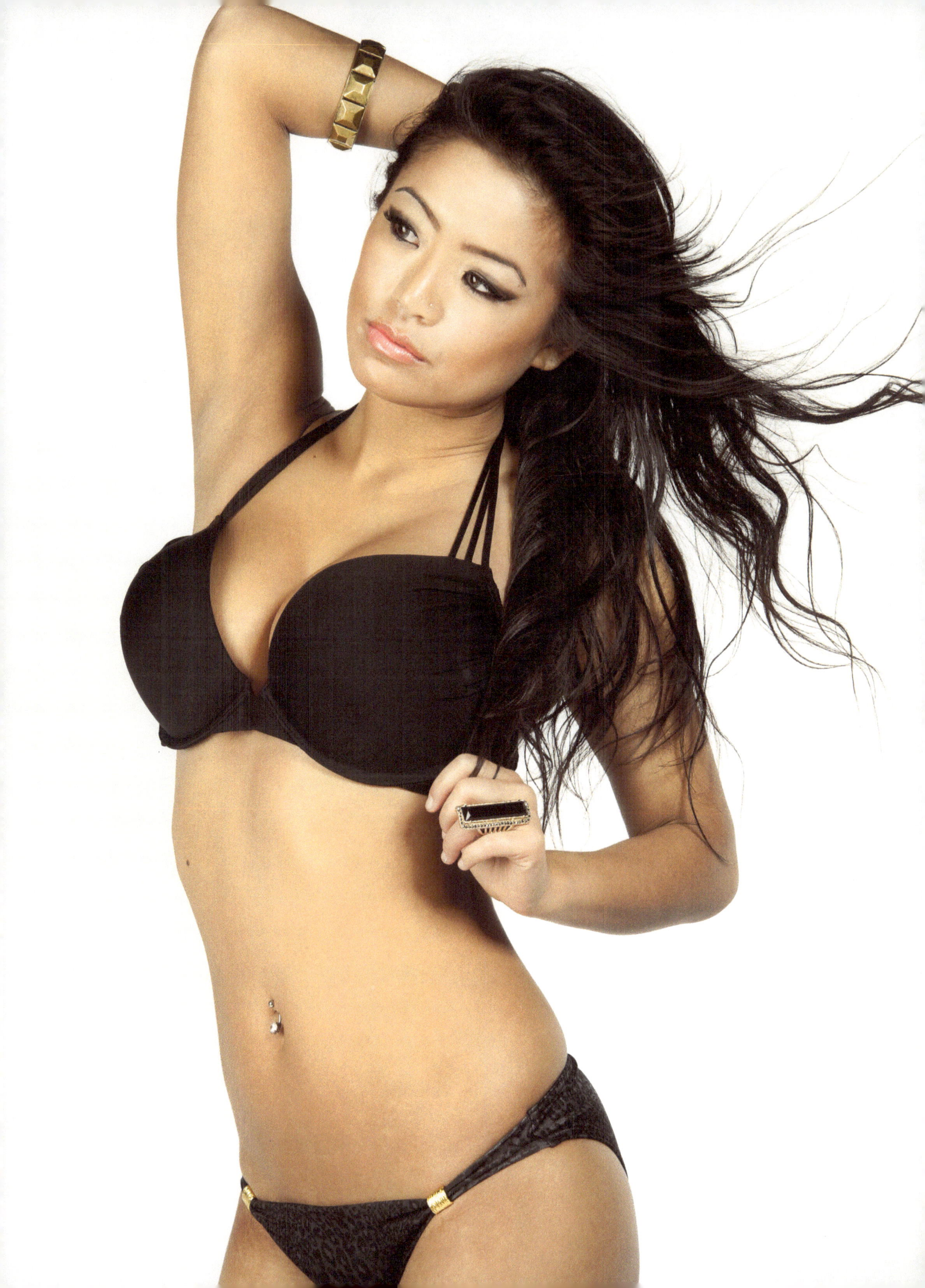

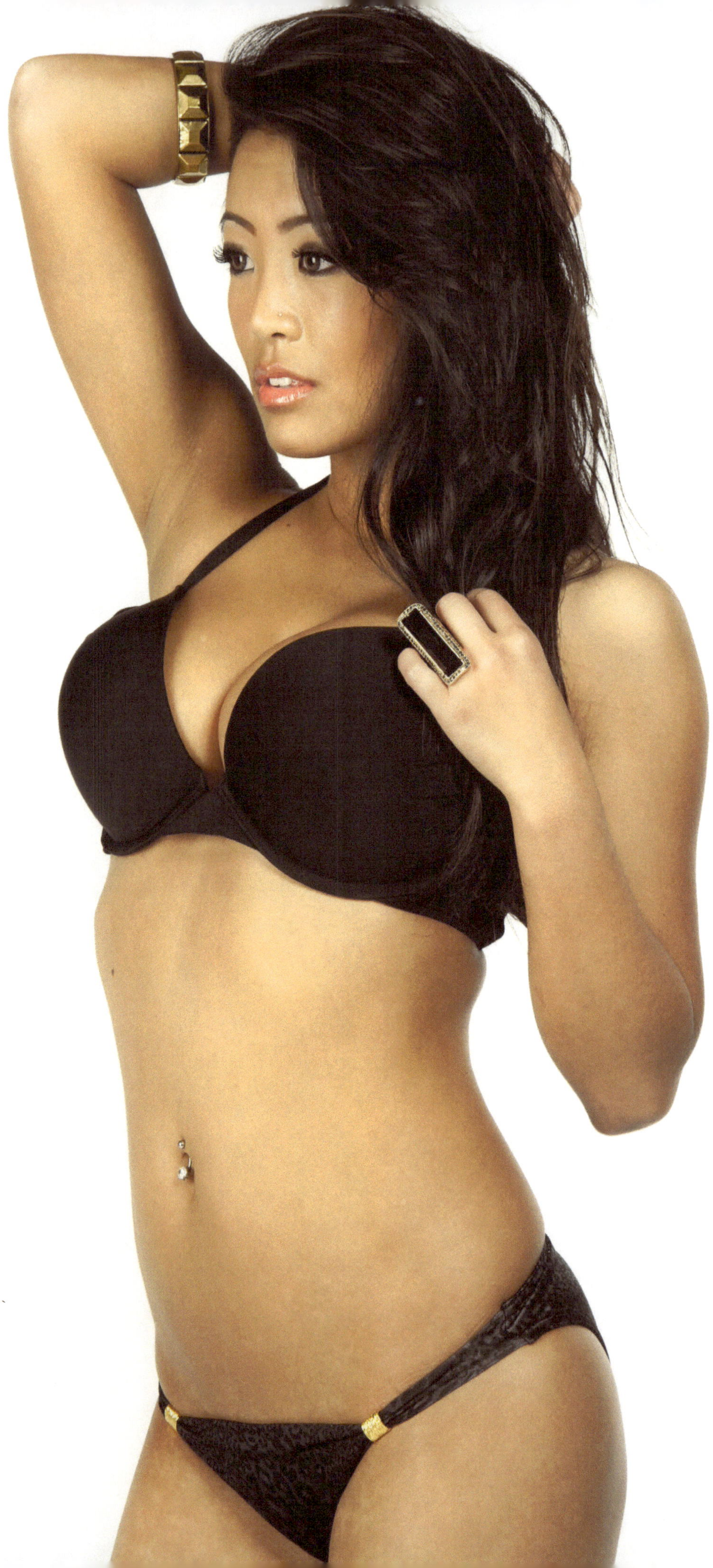

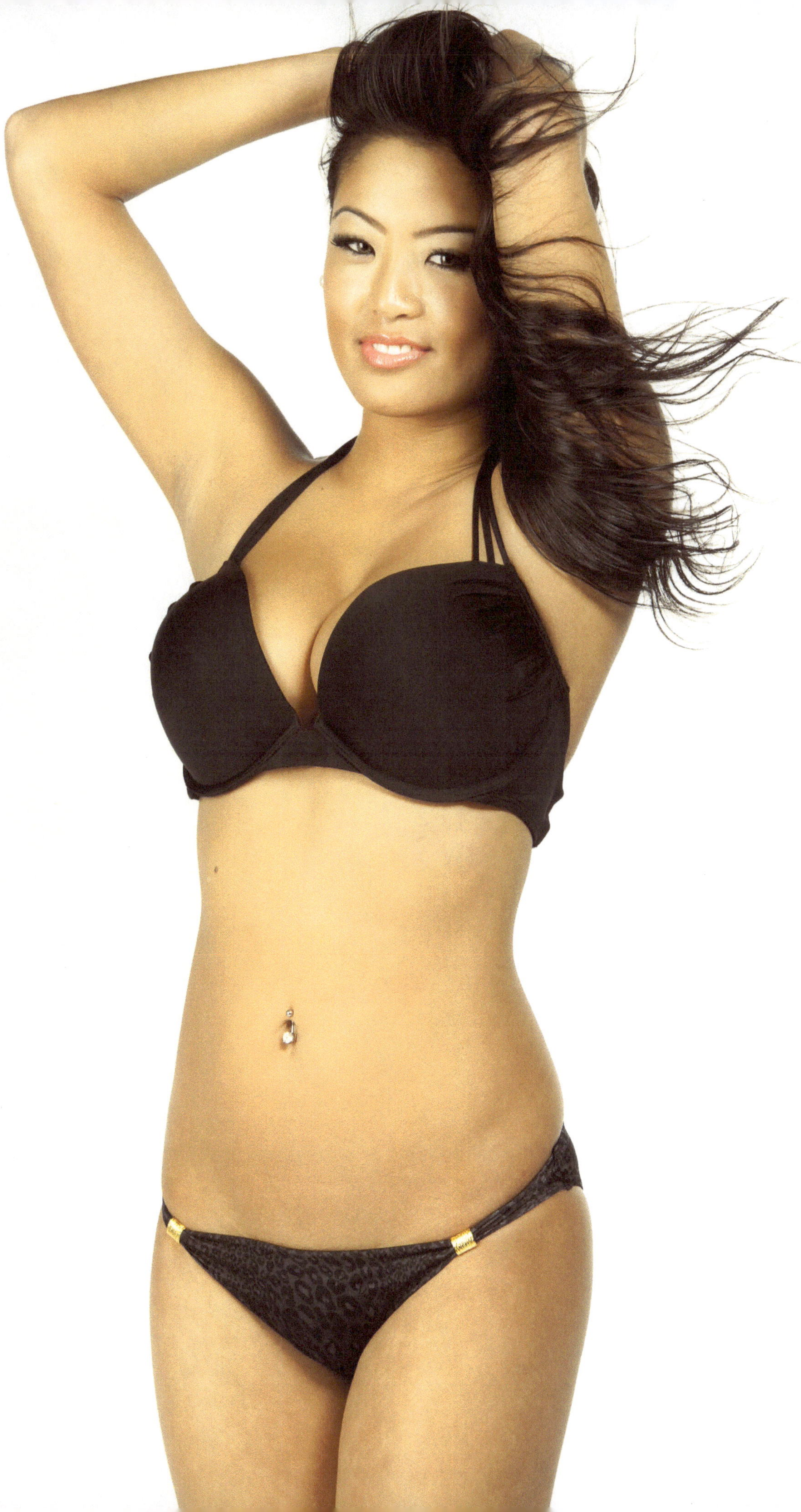

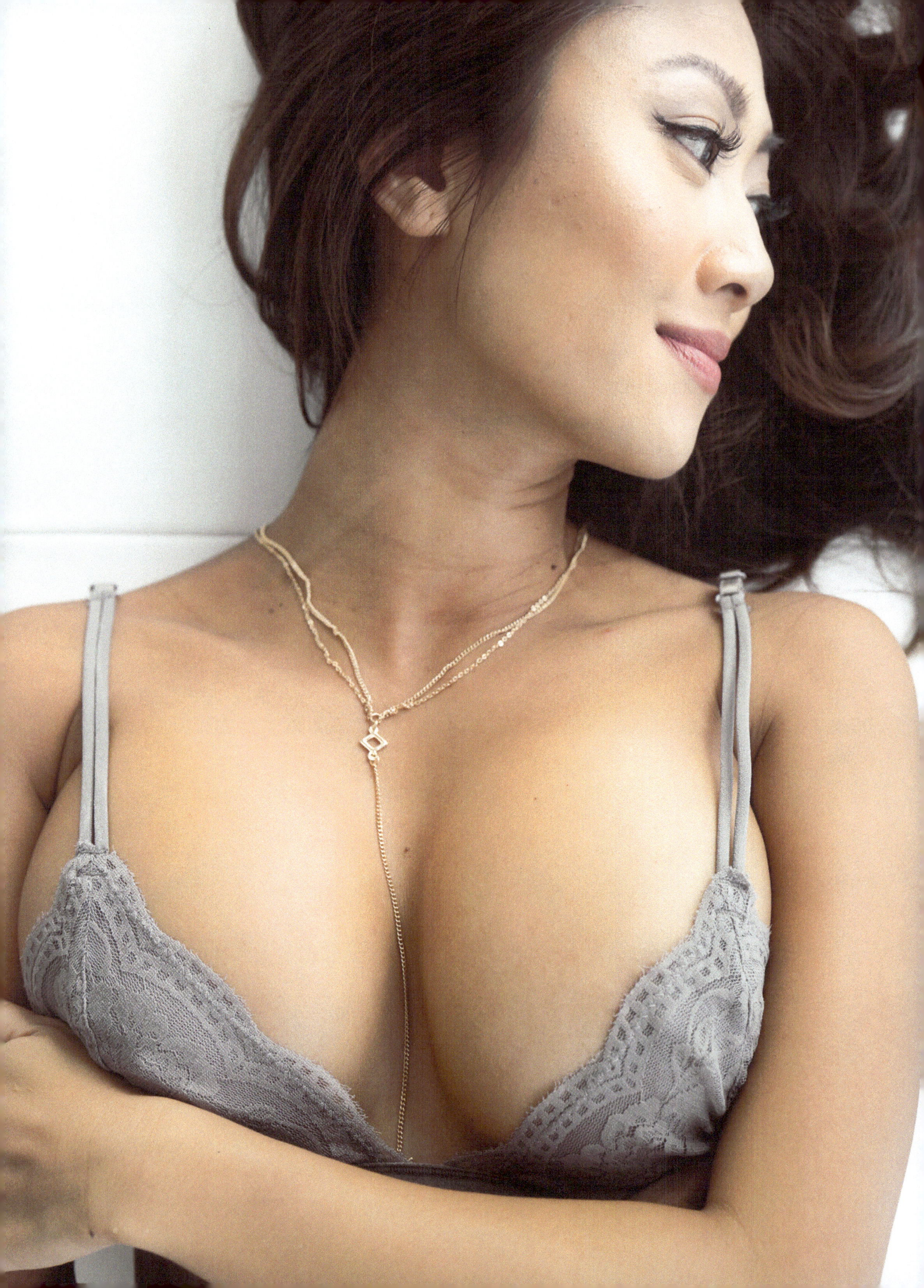

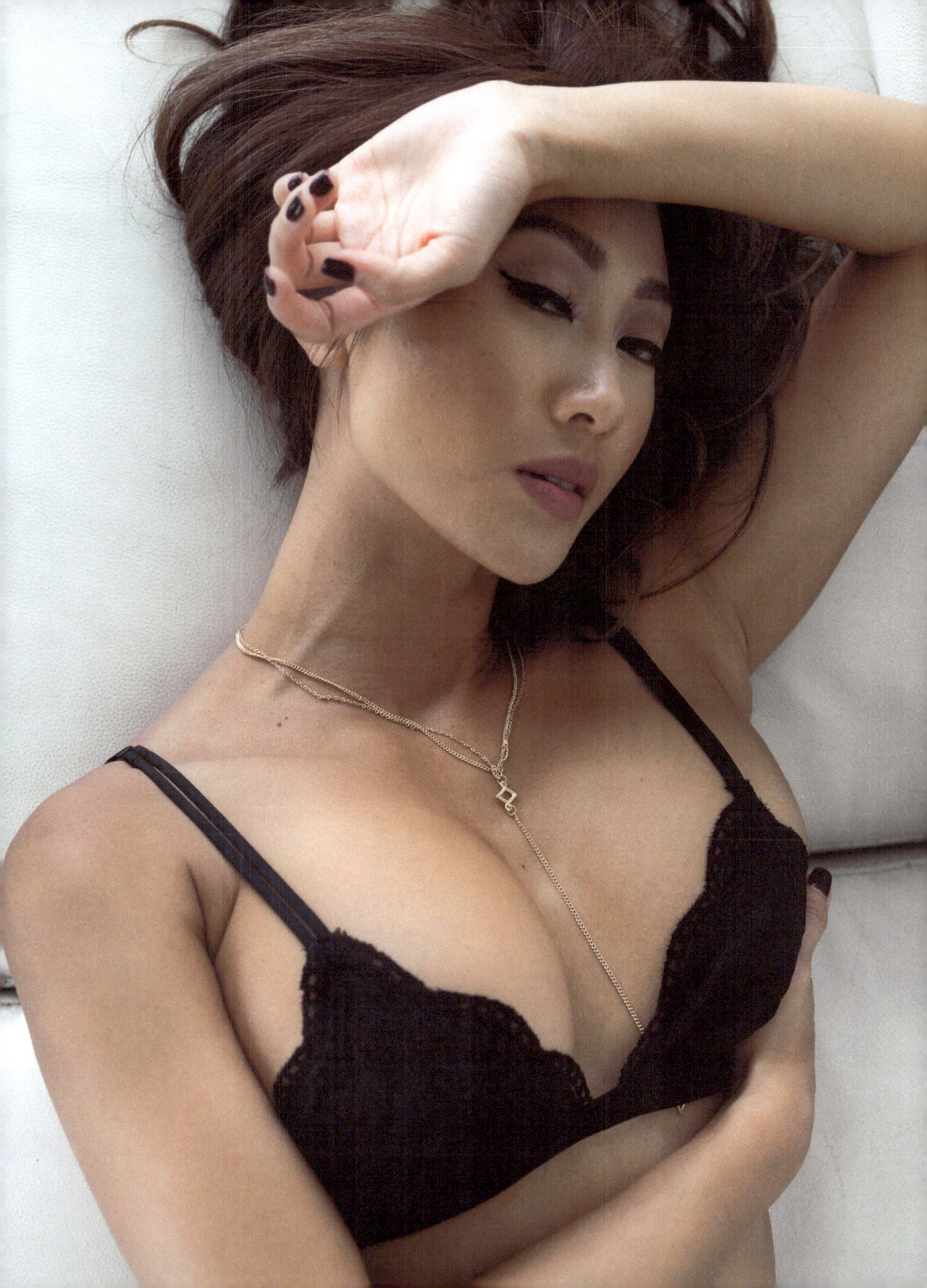

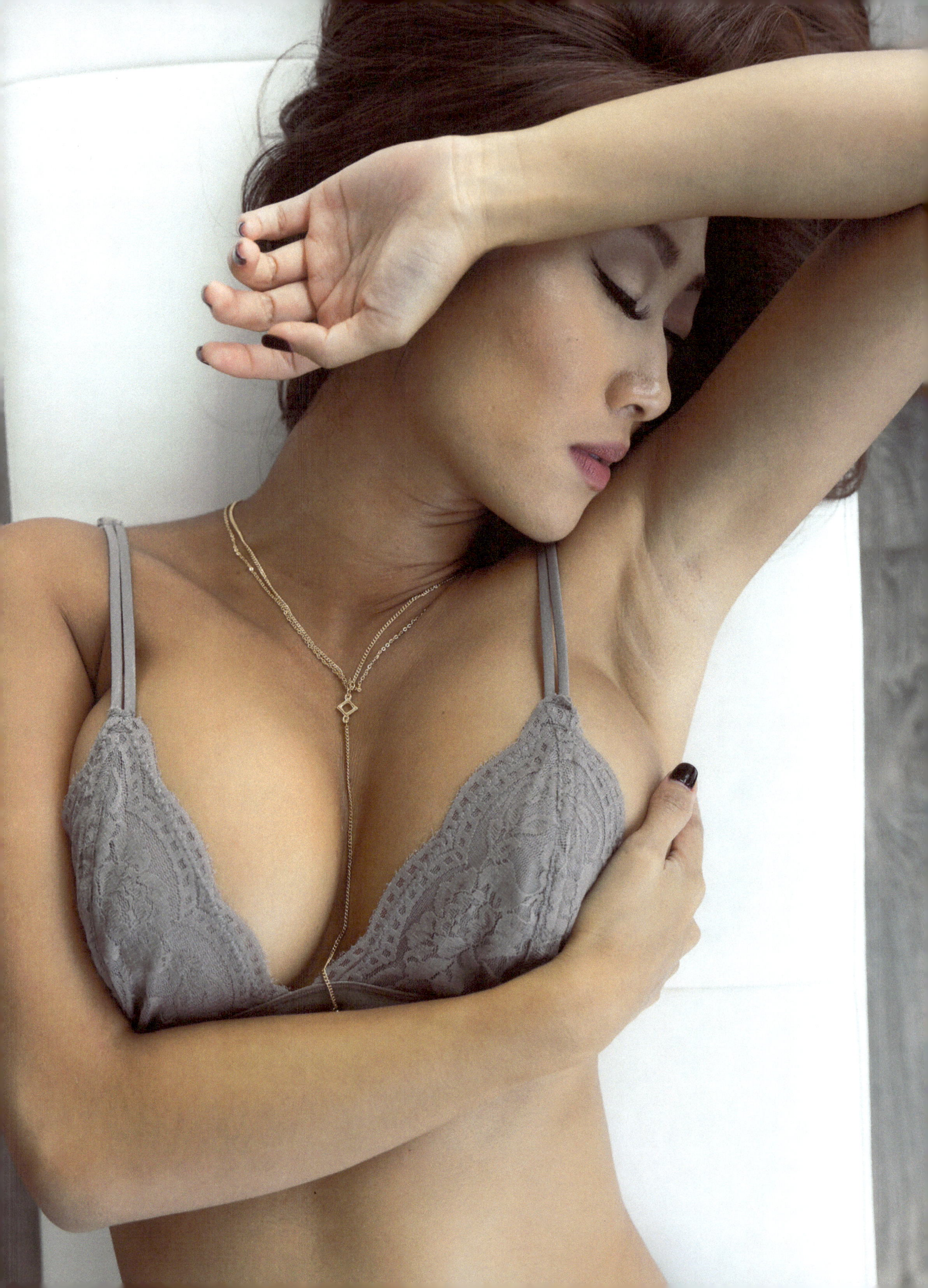

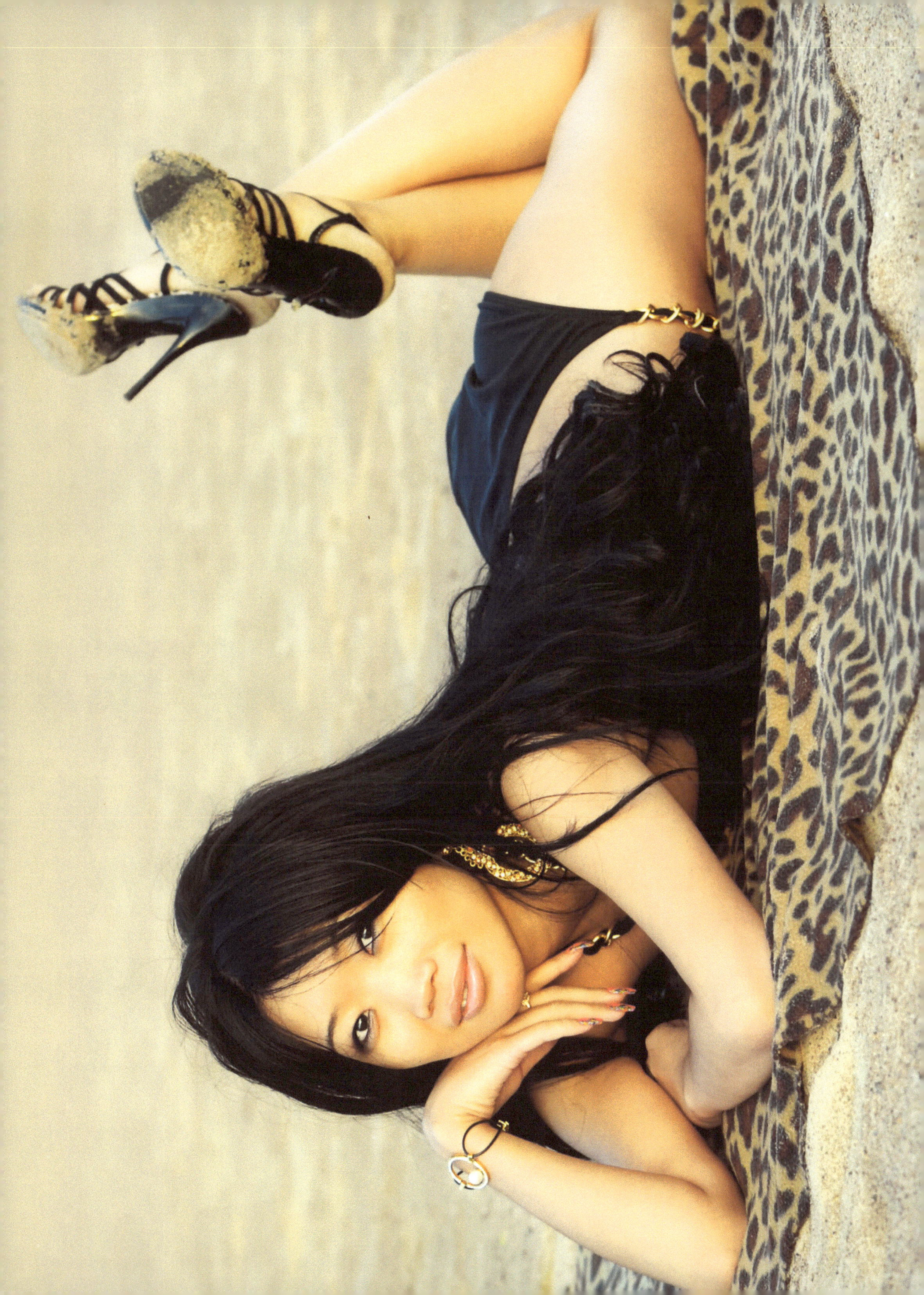

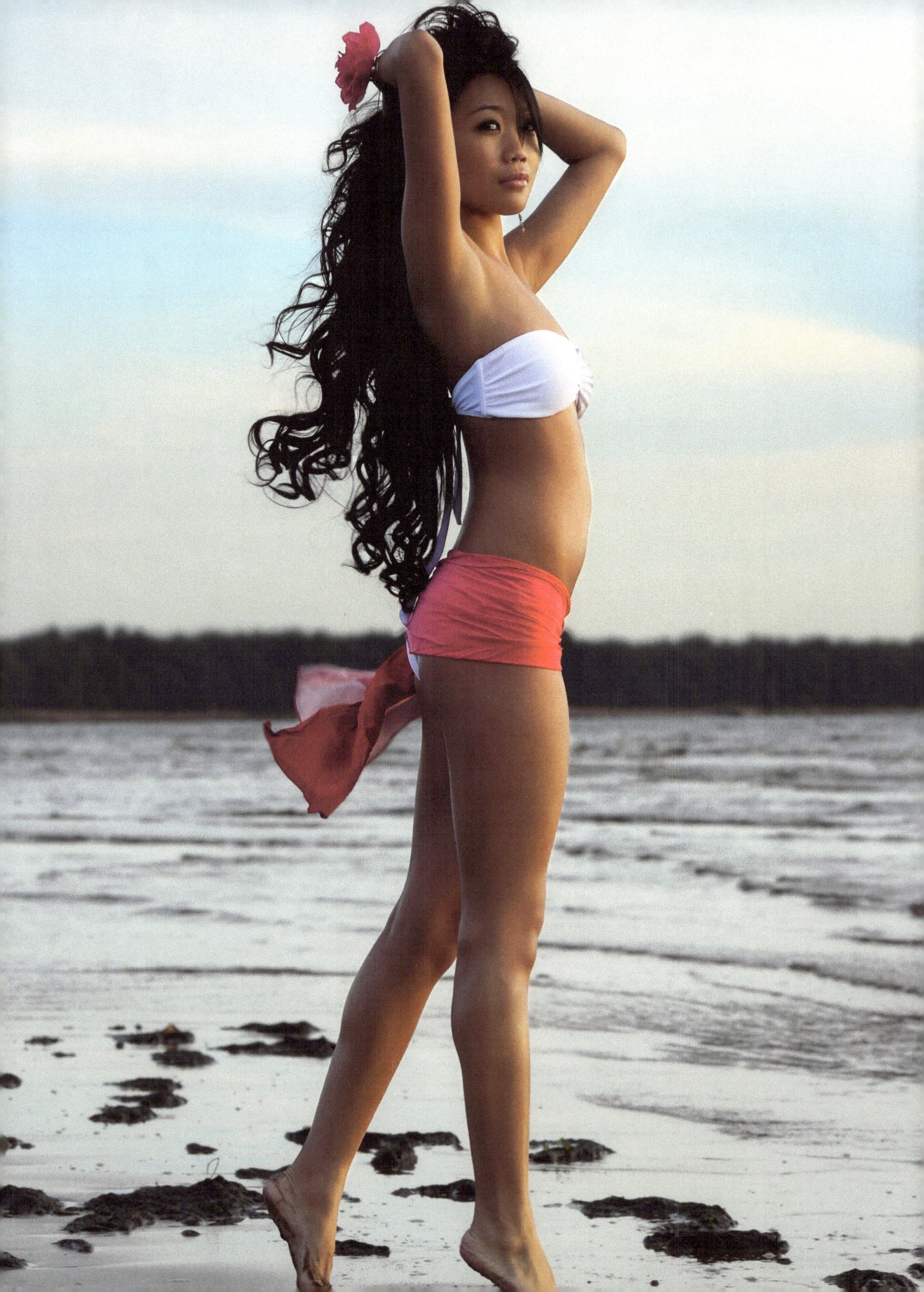

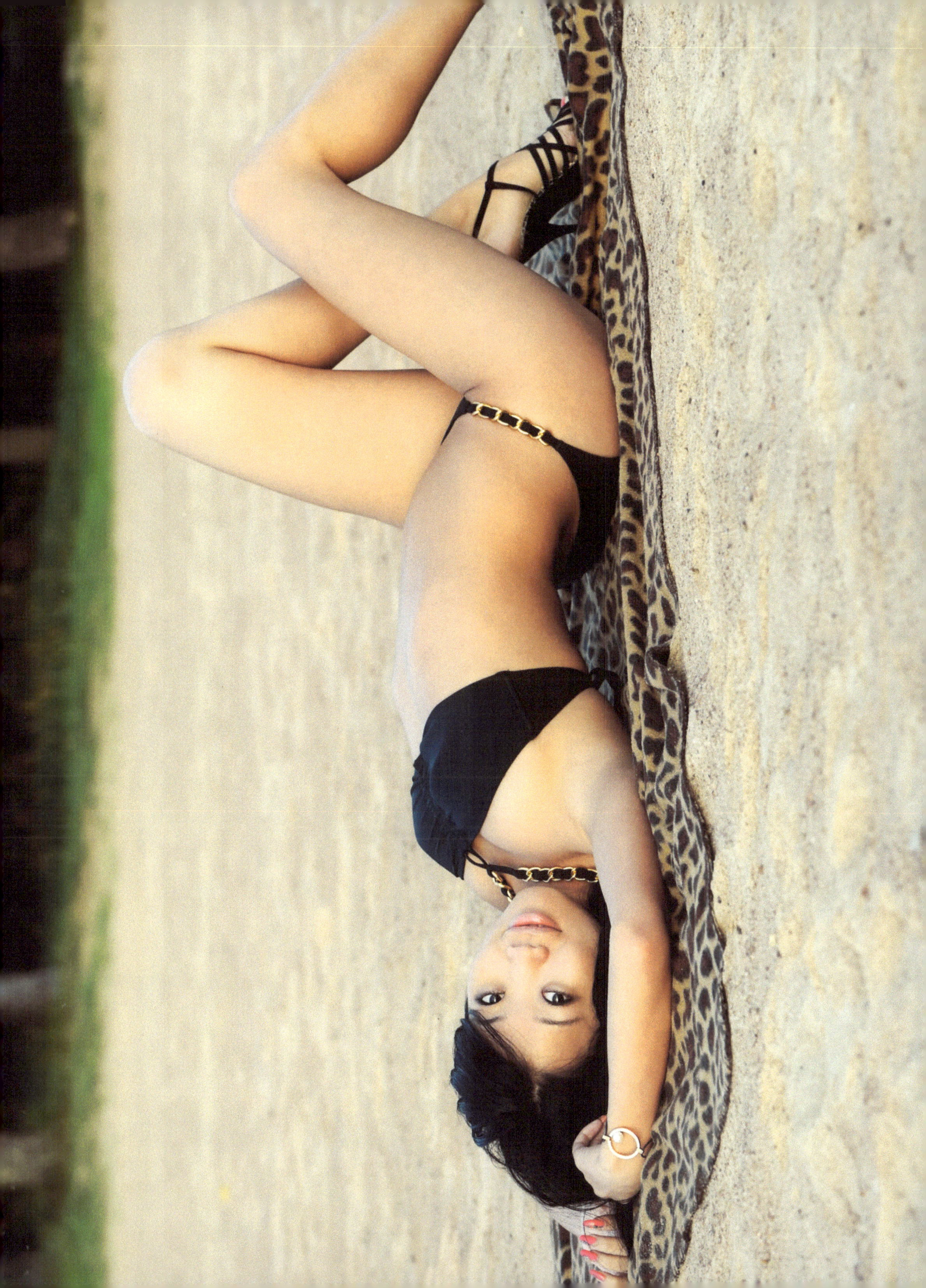

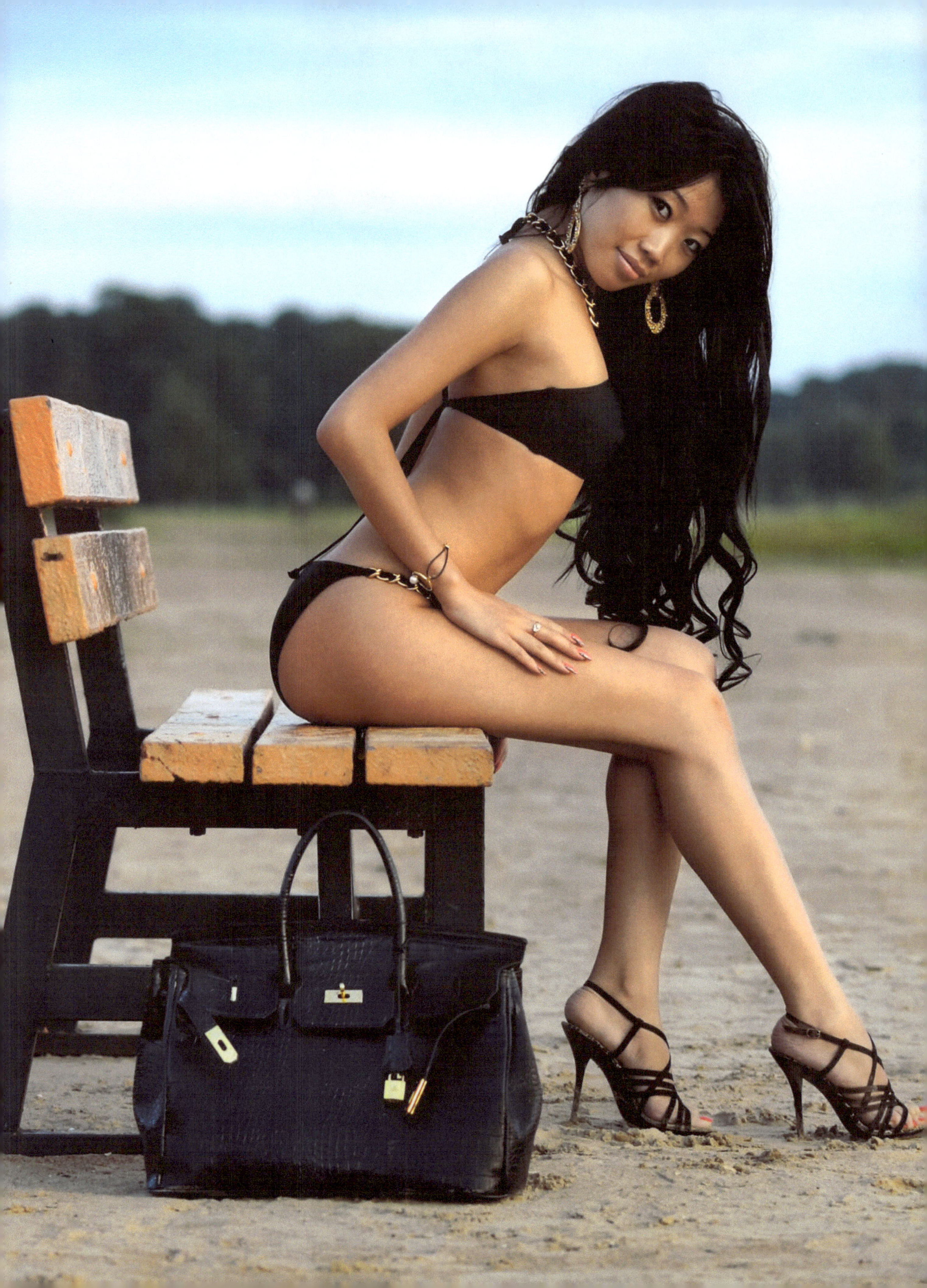

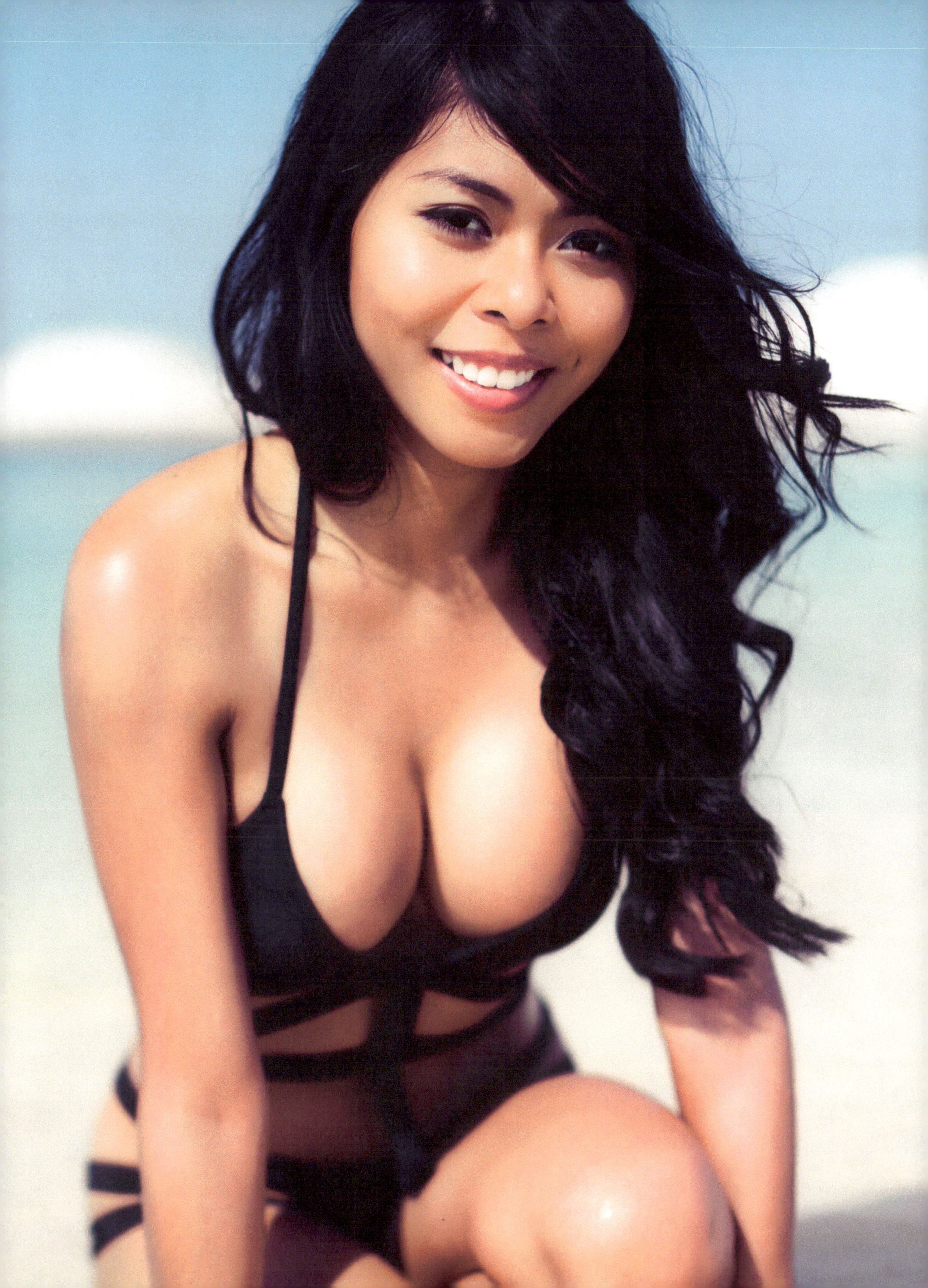

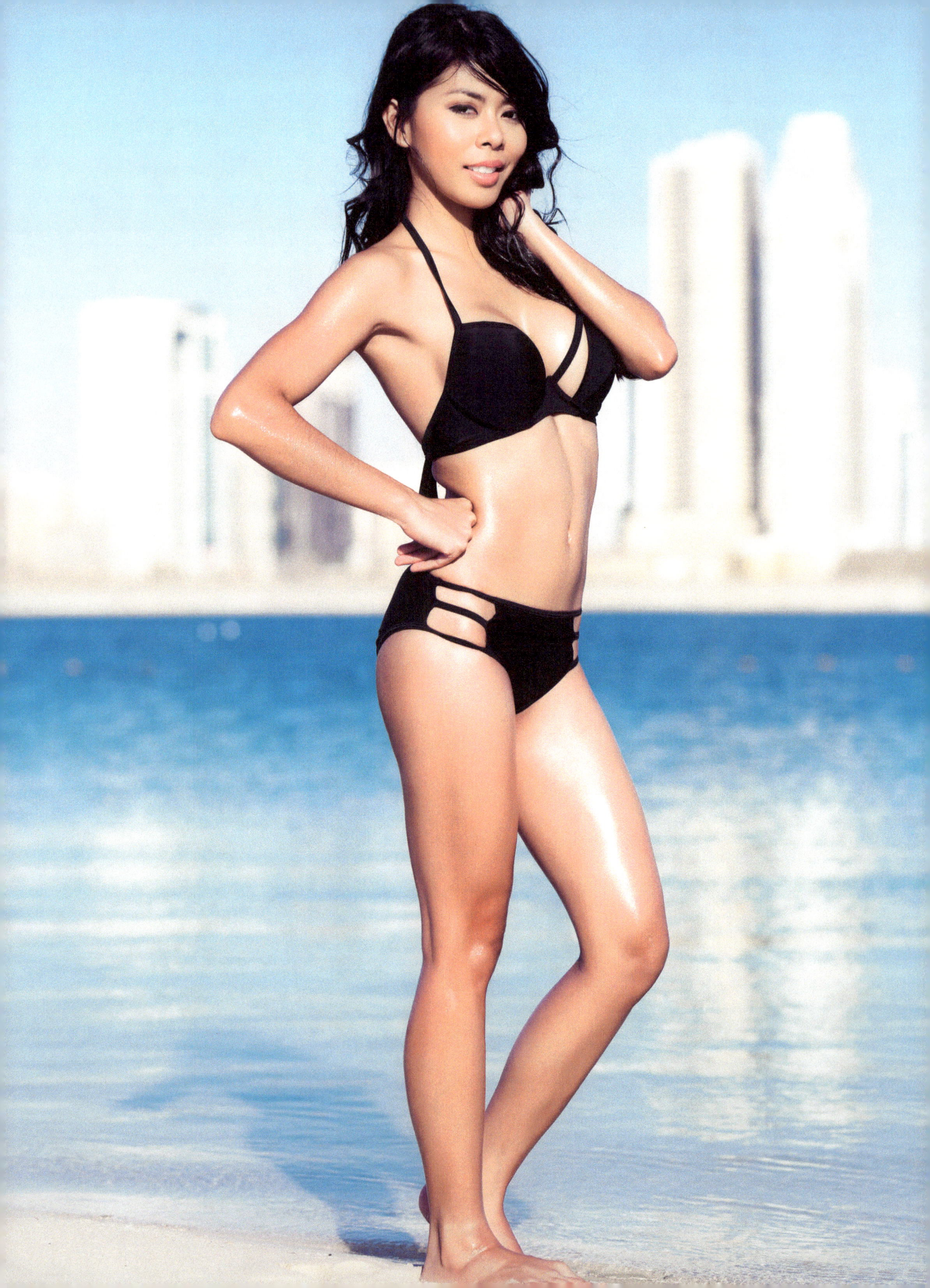

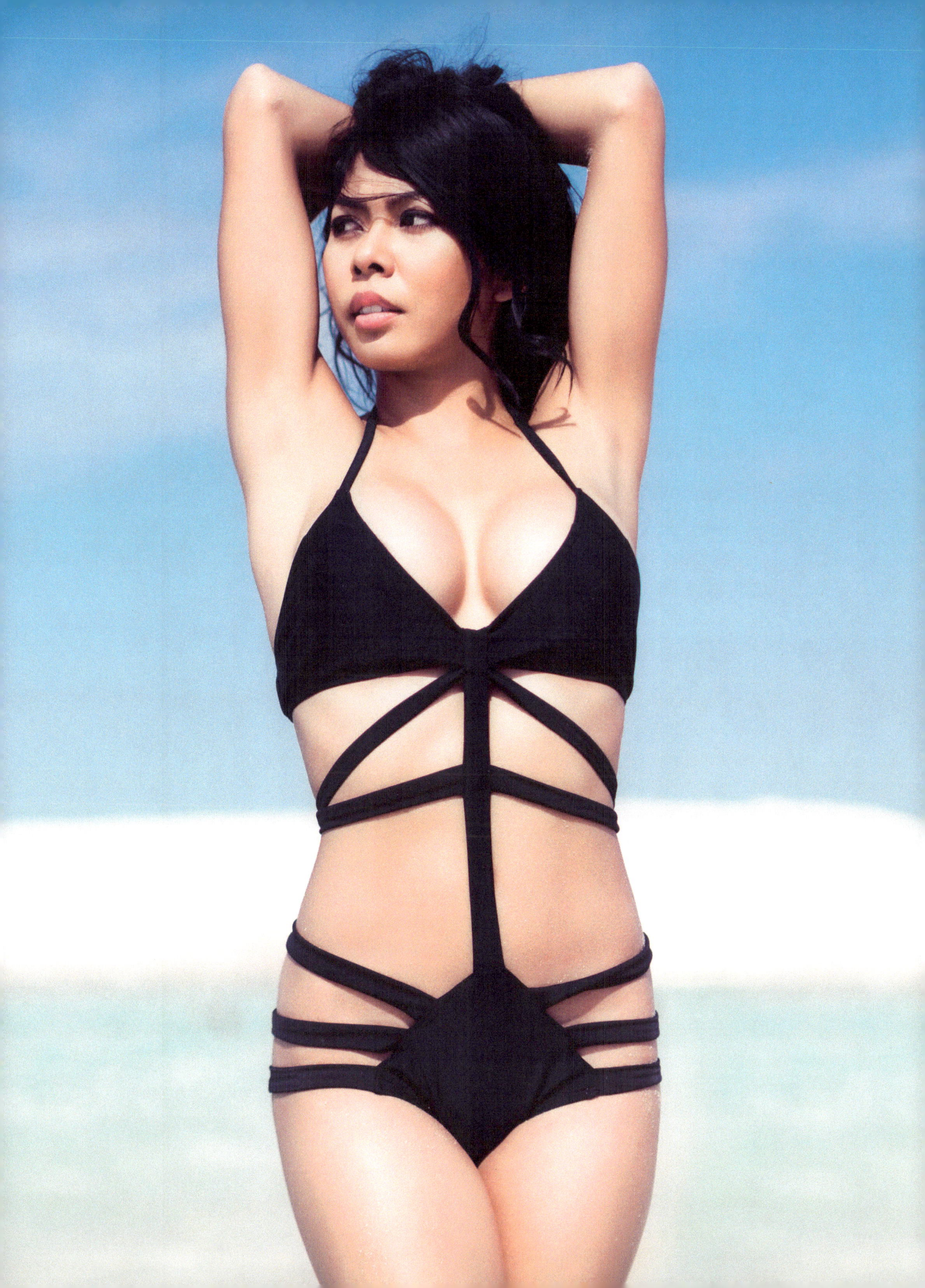

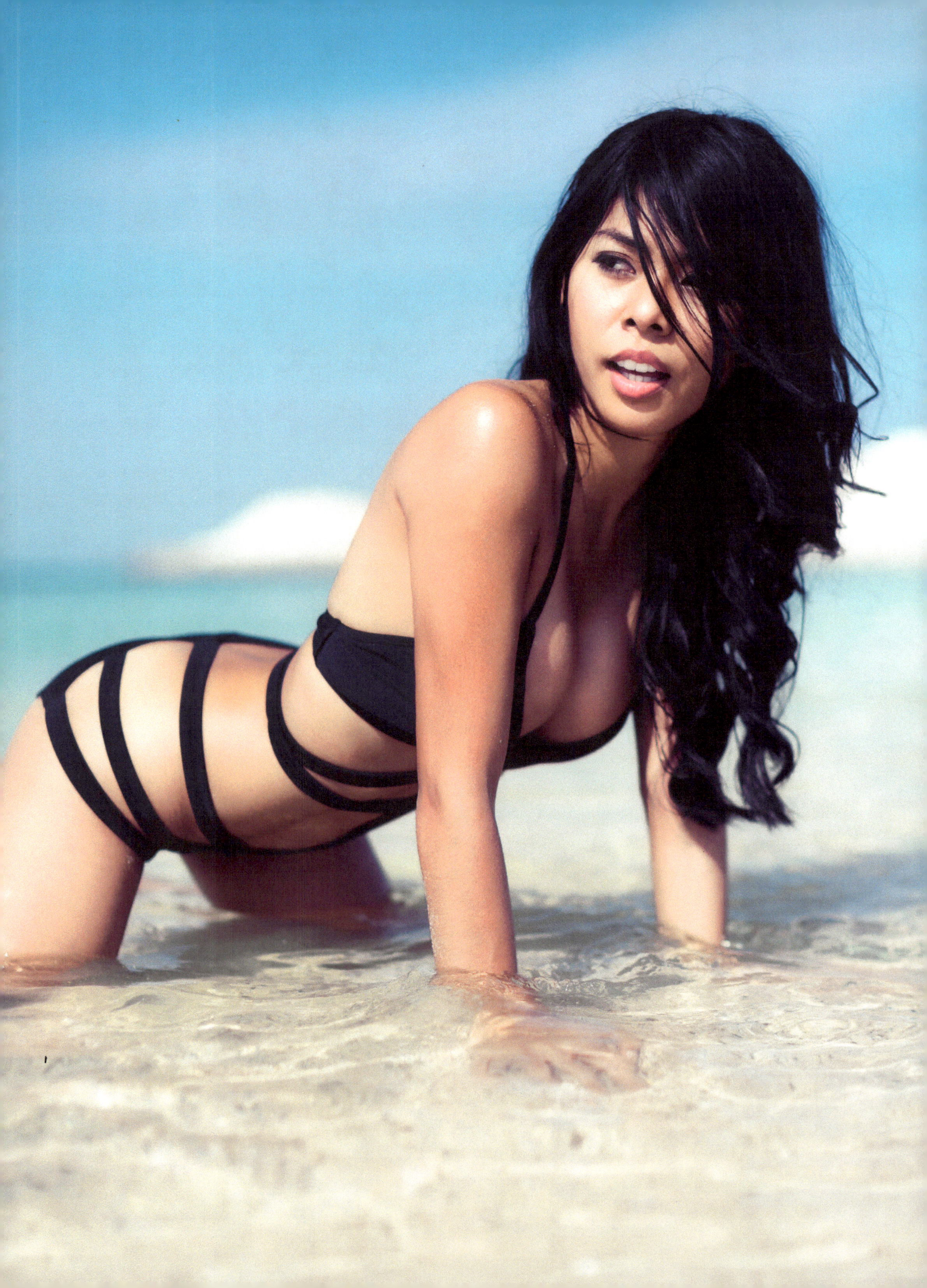

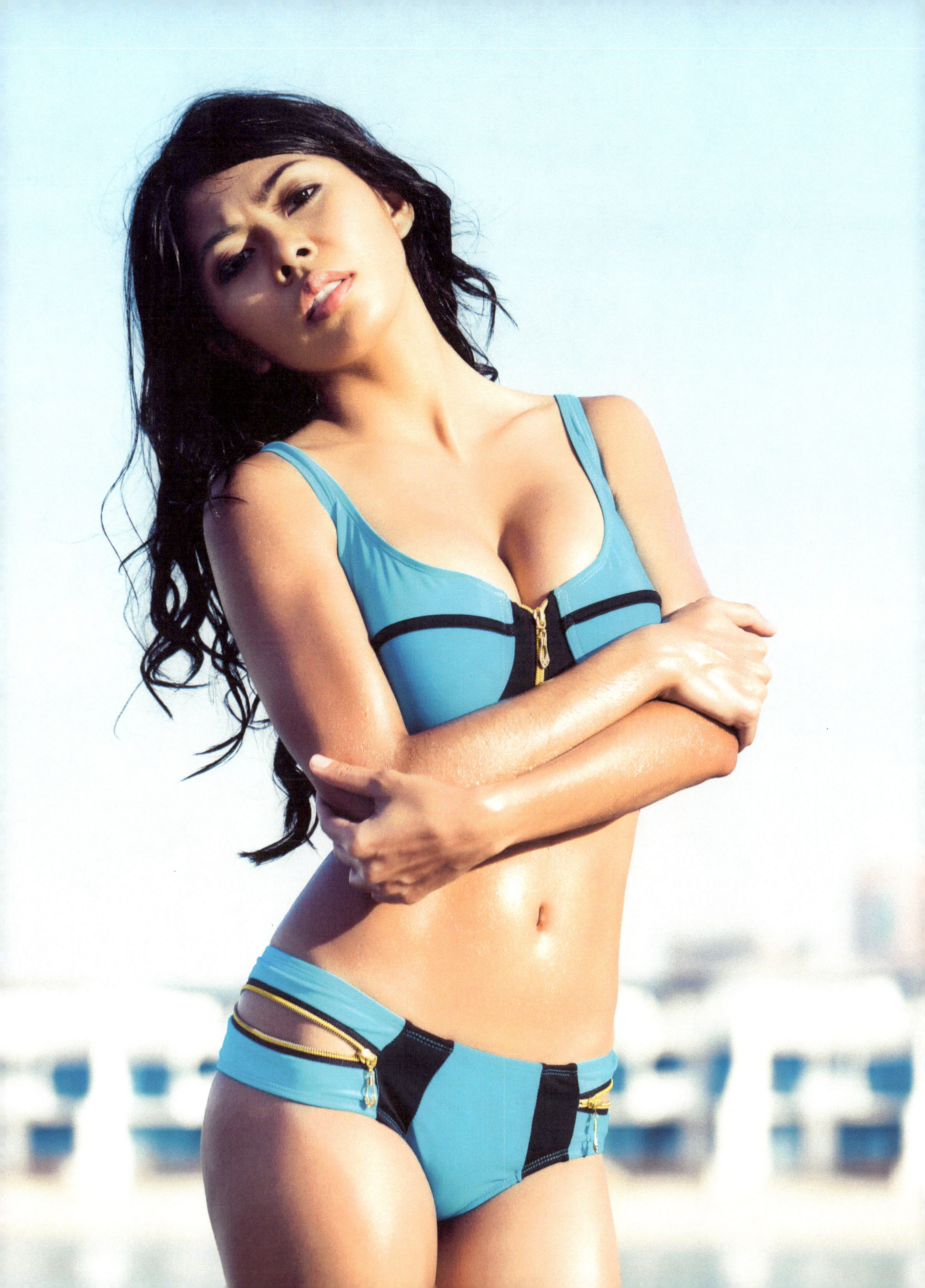

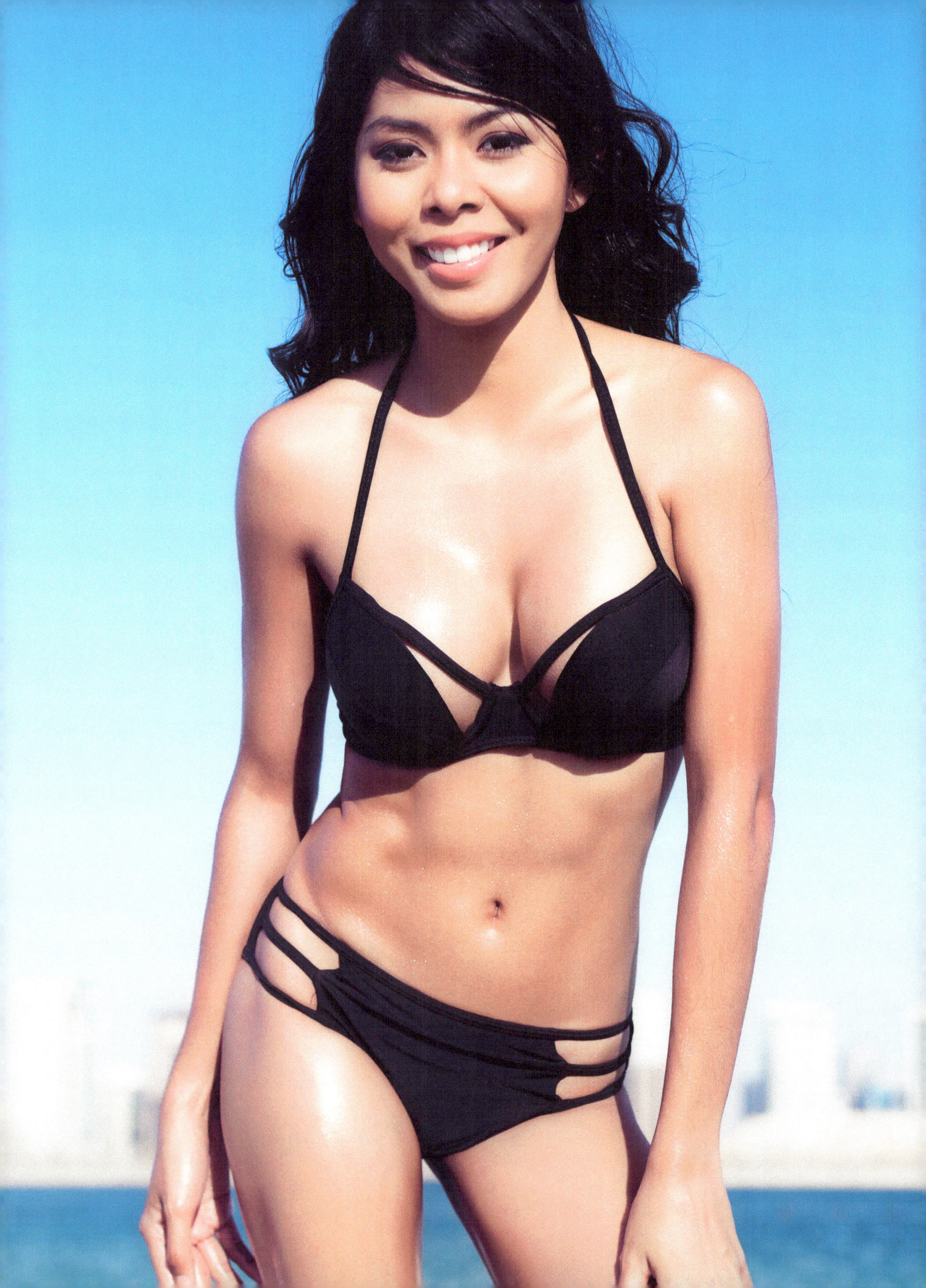

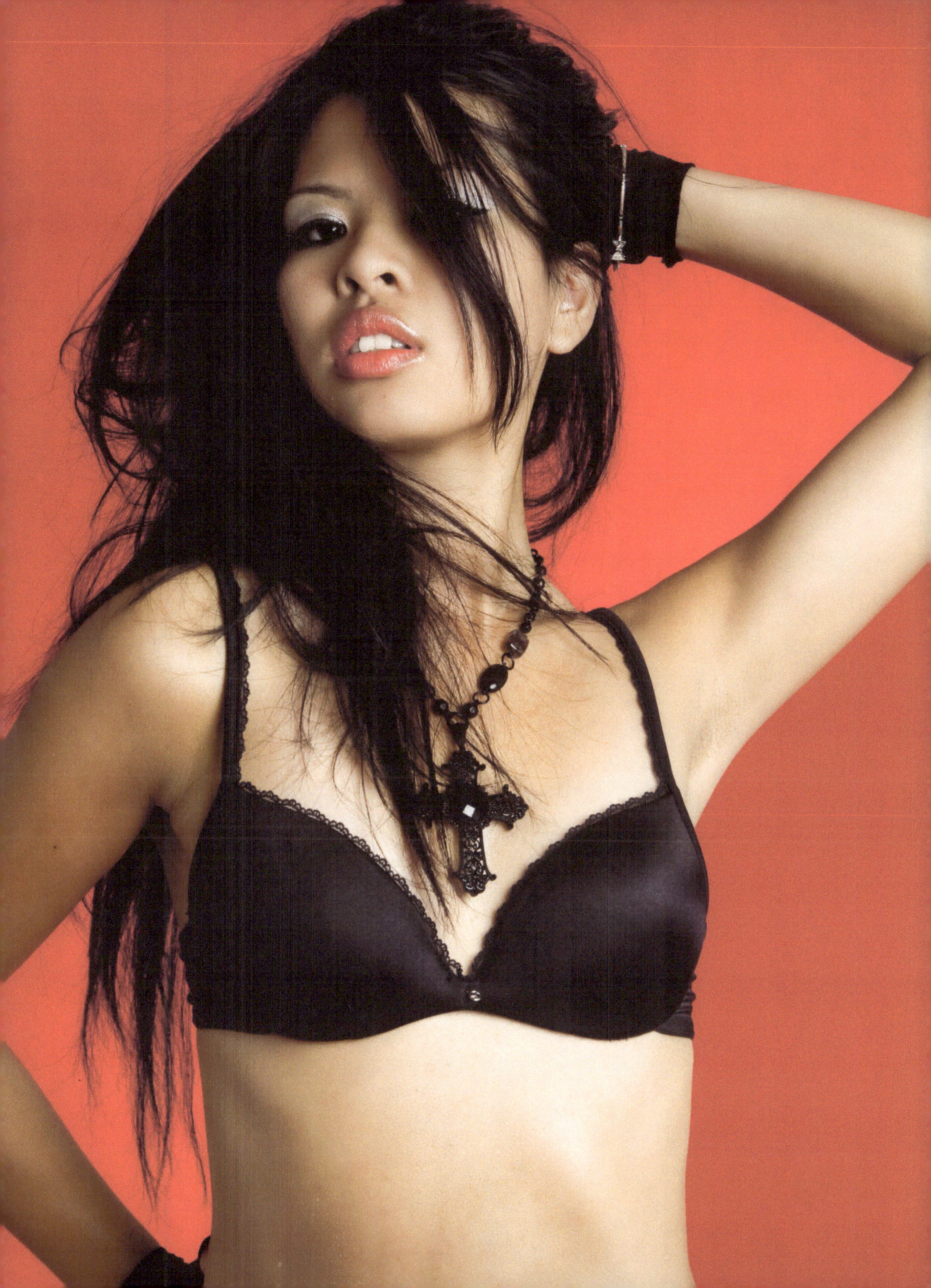

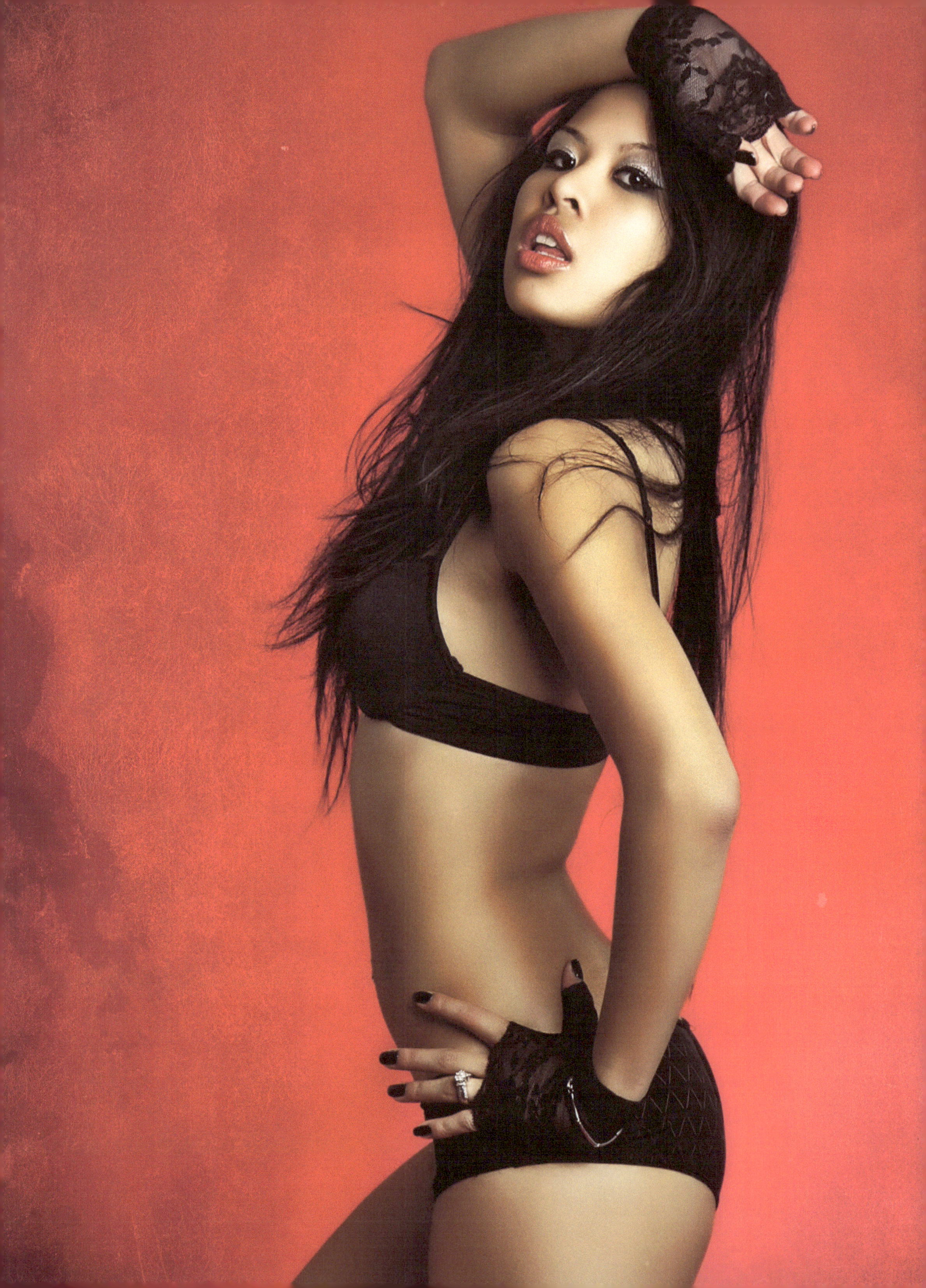

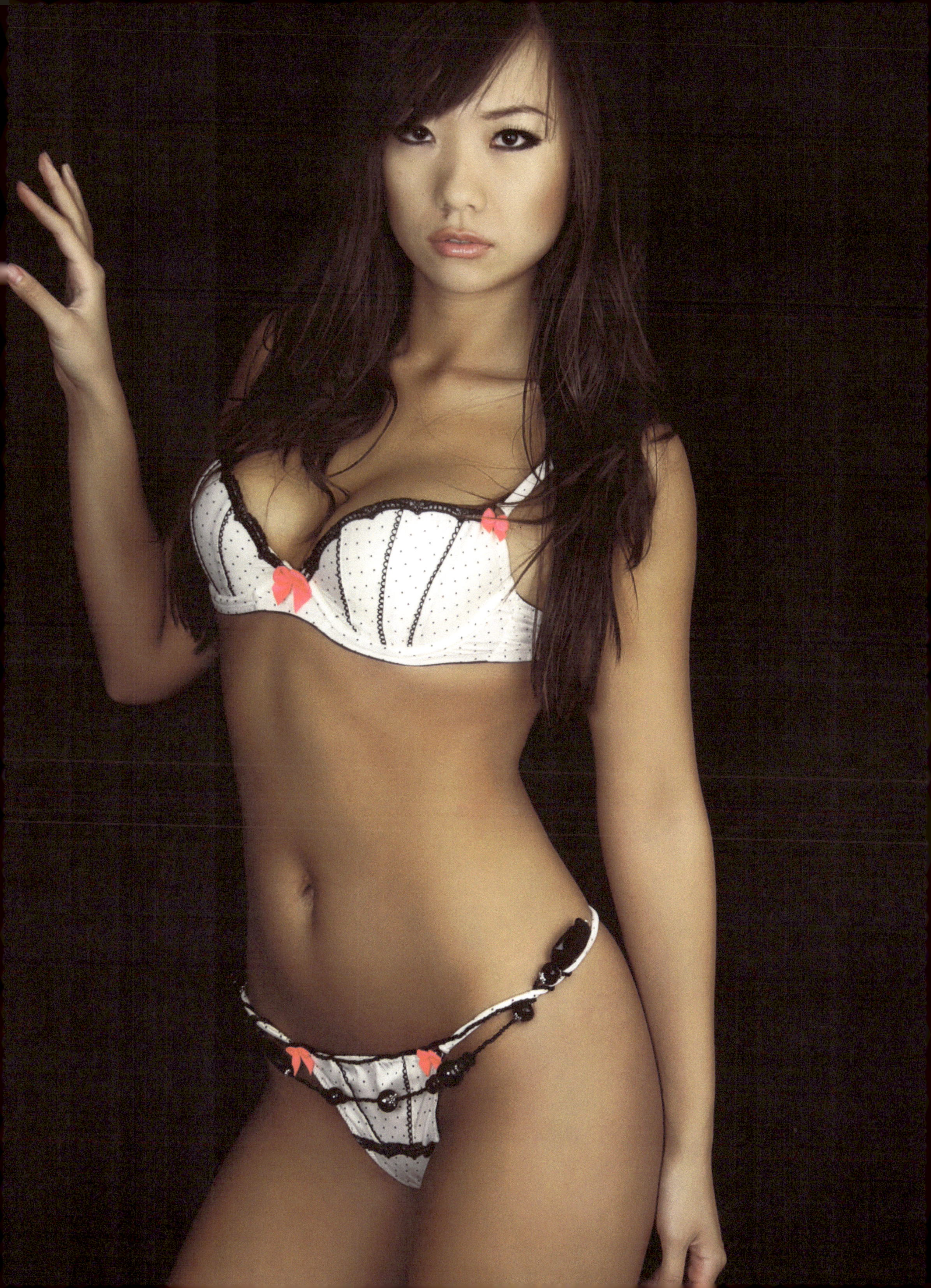

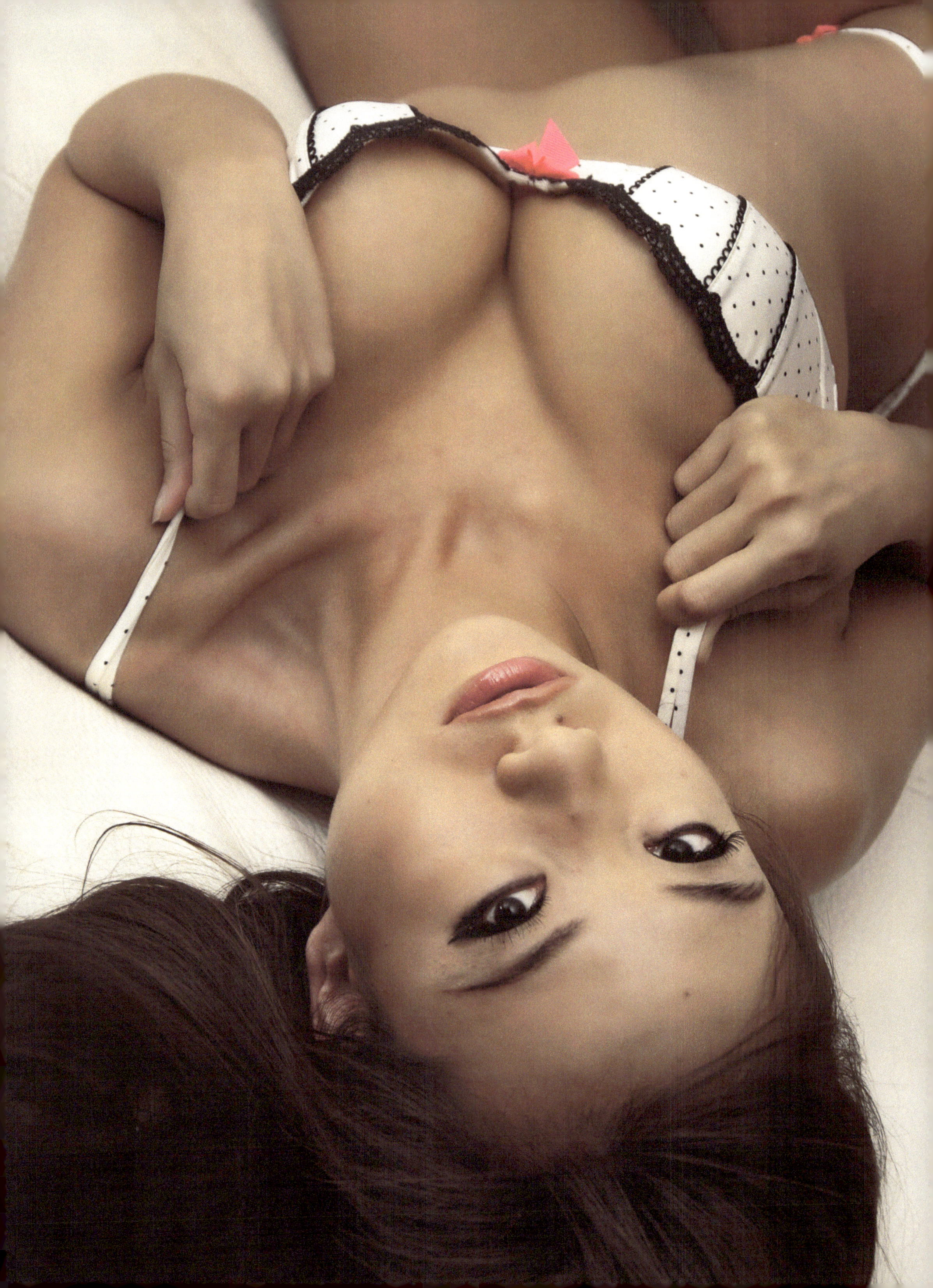

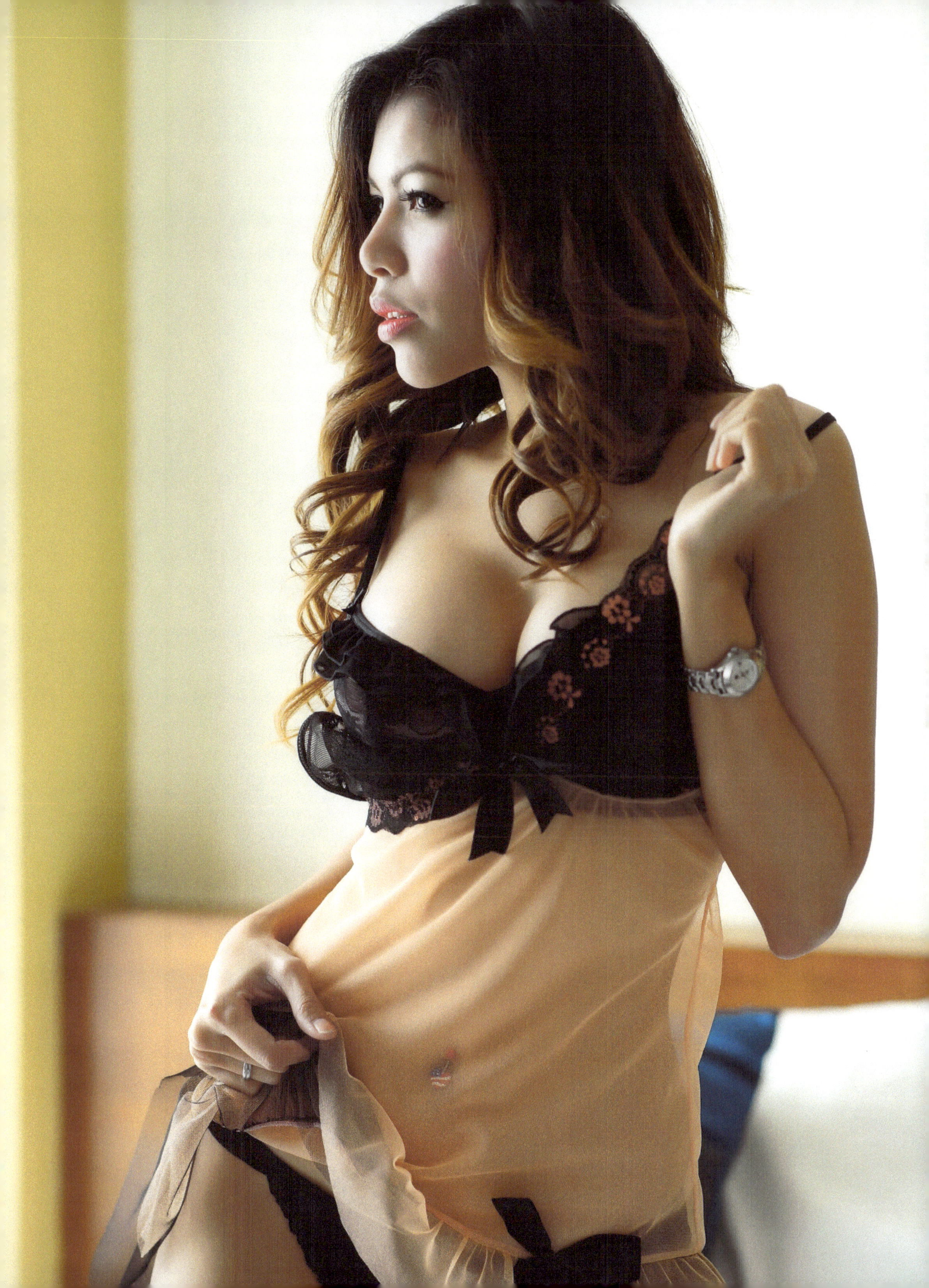

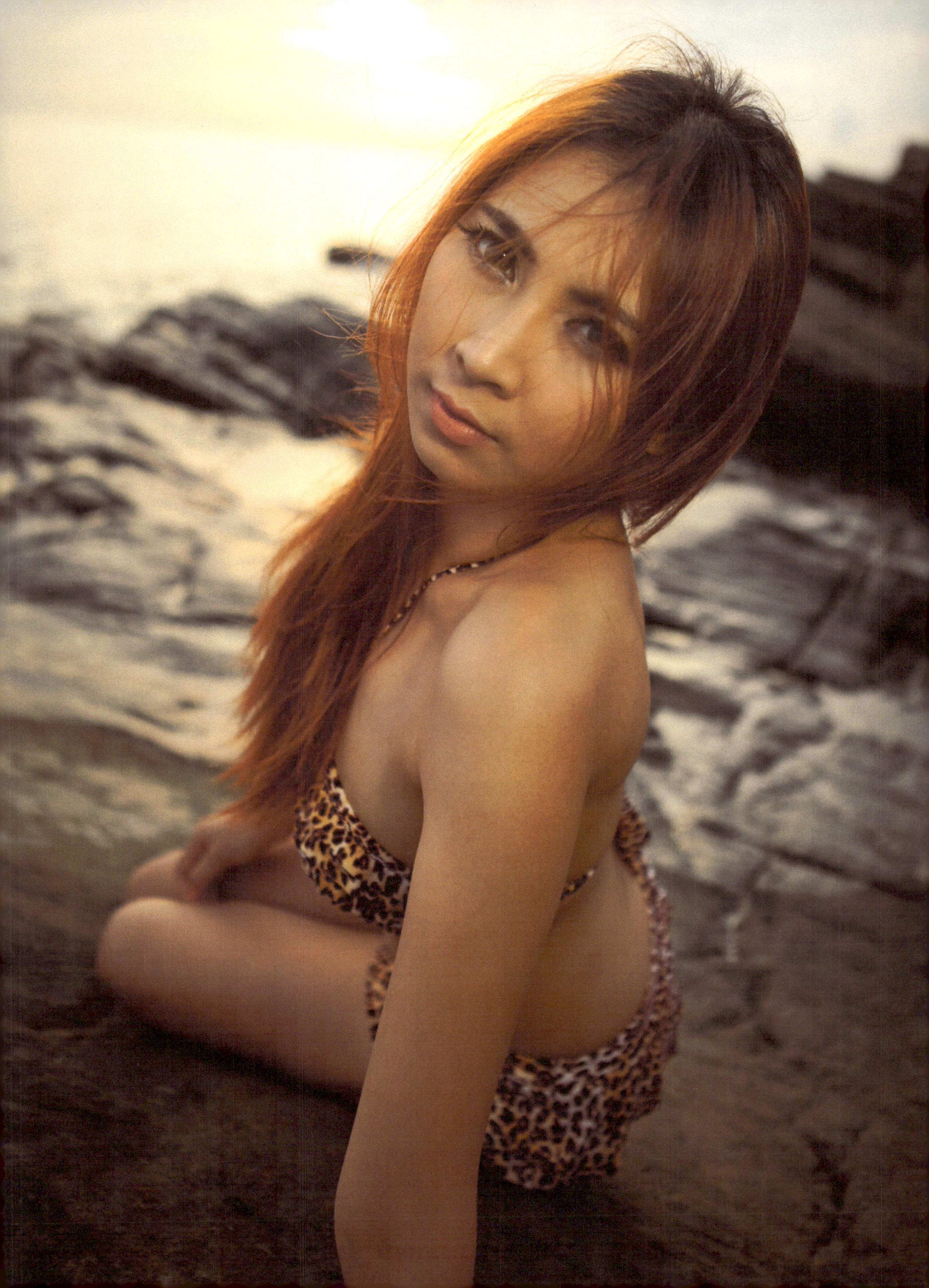

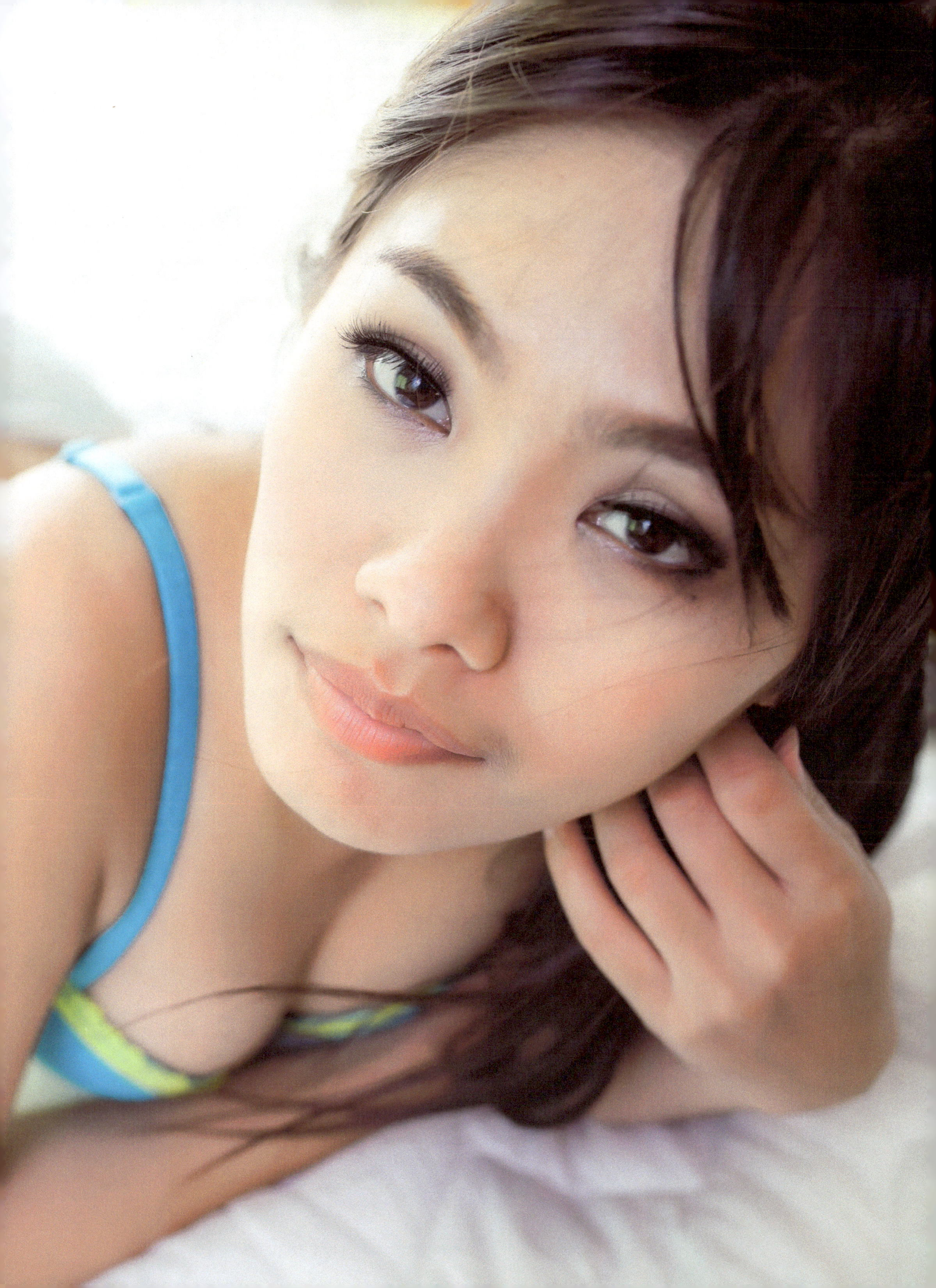

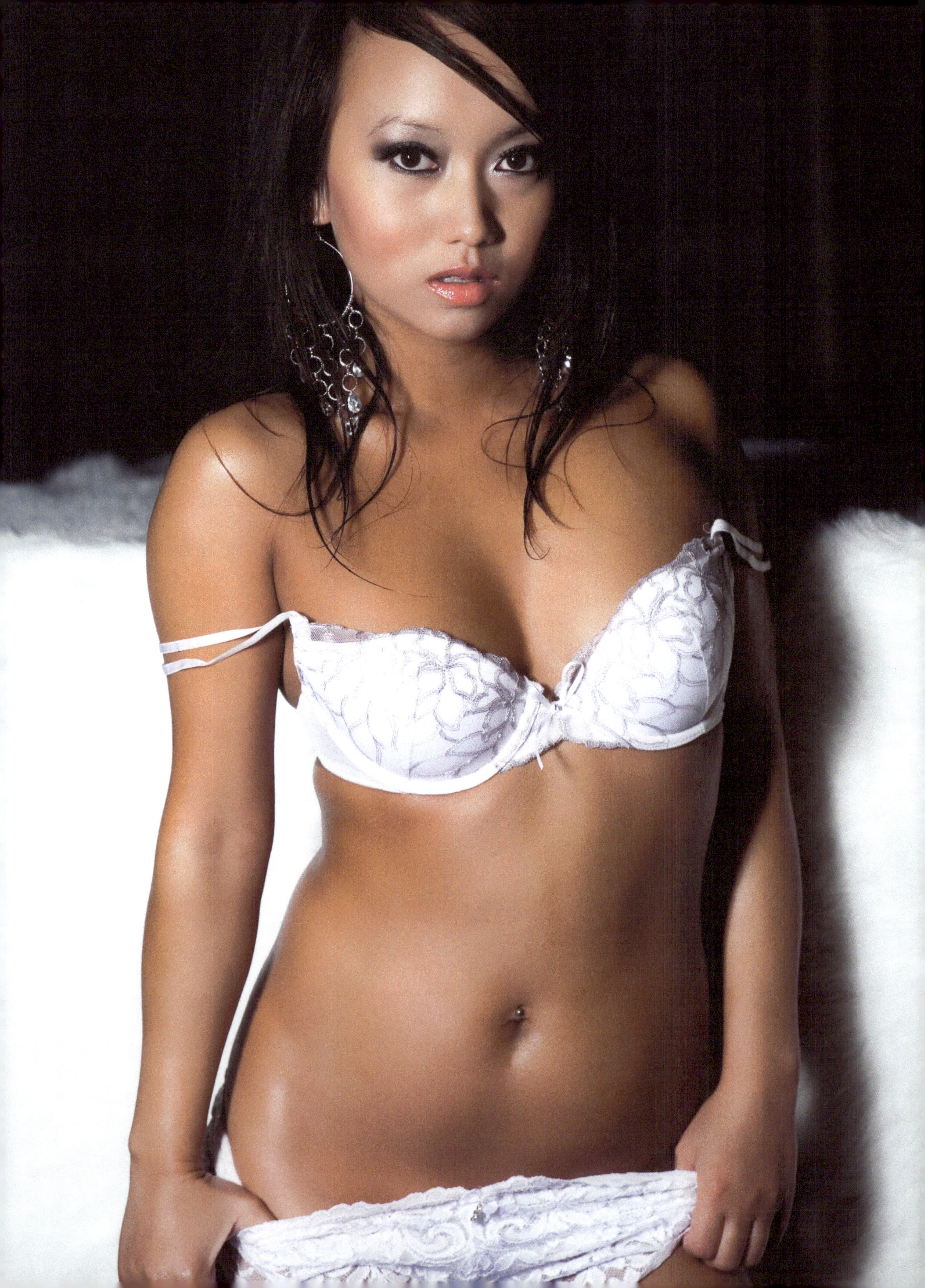

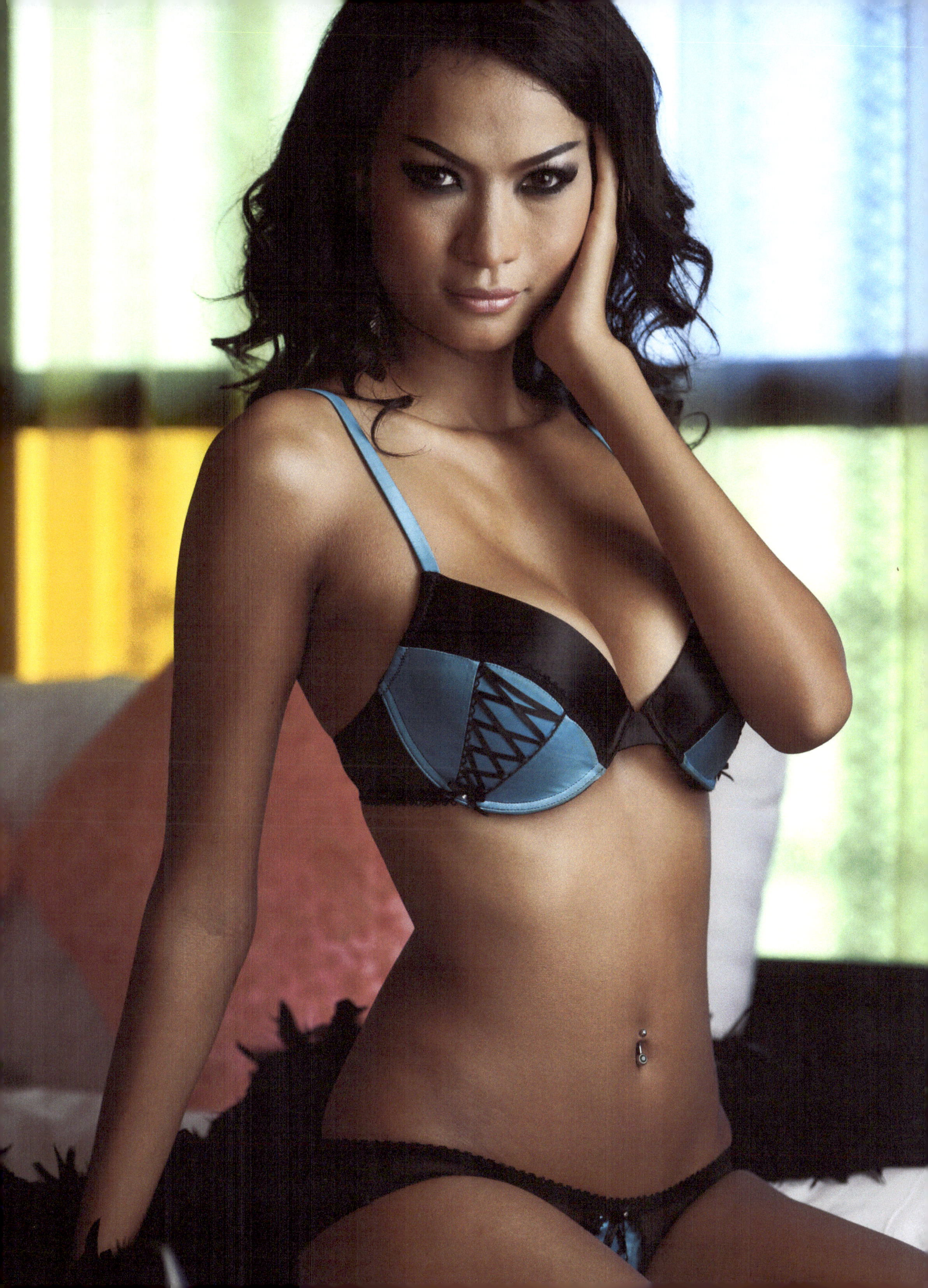

www.ingramcontent.com/pod-product-compliance
Lightning Source LLC
Chambersburg PA
CBHW050419180526
45159CB00005B/2331
* 9 7 8 1 5 3 9 0 9 5 4 9 1 *